How To Tie & Untie Mist

How To Tie & Untie Mist

Daniel Hales

Frayed Edge Press
Philadelphia, PA
2025

Copyright 2025 Daniel Hales

Published by Frayed Edge Press in 2025

Frayed Edge Press
Philadelphia, PA 19101

http://frayededgepress.com

Cover collages by Daniel Hales
Graphic design by James Lowe
Author photo by Dan Little

Publisher's Cataloging-in-Publication

Names: Hales, Daniel.
Title: How to tie & untie mist / Daniel Hales.
Other titles: How to tie and untie mist.
Description: Philadelphia, PA : Frayed Edge Press, 2025.
Identifiers: LCCN 2025934209 | ISBN 9781642510638 (pbk.) | ISBN
   9781642510652 (Kindle)
Subjects: LCSH: Questions and answers – Poetry. | Conduct of life – Poetry. |
   BISAC: POETRY / American / General. | POETRY / Subjects & Themes / General.
Classification: LCC PS3608.A447 C66 2025 | DDC 811 H--dc23
LC record available at https://lccn.loc.gov/2025934209

How To Find What You're Looking For

&&&

How To Read This	3
How To Find Redemption	4
How To Perform Miracles & Make Wishes Come True	5
How To Deliver Our Elevator Pitch	6
How To Raise Your Action	7
How To Get On First Base	8
How To Approach A Swan	9
How To Light A Candle	10
How To Give It A Name, 3	11
How To Pronounce My Name	12-13
How To Get A Promotion	14
How To Resign	15-16
How To Win The Spring Offensive	17
How To Break Answers	18
How To Exceed Impossible Expectations	19-26
How To Pray	27-28

&&

How To Make A New Year's Resolution	31
How To Make A Sandwich, 2	32
How To Disenchant A Passerine	33
How To Make A Sandwich, 1	34
How To Pass Through Walls	35
How To Play	36
How To Fulfill The Prophecy	37
How To Disappear Completely	38
How To Give It A Name, 2	39-41
How To Haunt Your House	42

How To Tie & Untie	43
How To Bow Your Heart	44
How To Tie & Untie A Tie	45
How To Climb The Pine At The End Of The Mind	46
How To Secure The Perimeter	47
How To Become An Ornitheologist	48
How To Die	49
How To Be Mist	50
How To Unread This	51

&

Re This	54
Red ion	55
How To live	56
First	57
Approach	58
and	59
Re	60
&	61
A New solution	62
How To appear Complete	63
&&	64
&&&	65
Mist	66
This	67

Who To Thank	71
Who To Blame	73

How To Tie & Untie Mist

&&&&&&&&&&&&&&&&&&&&&&&&&&&&&&&&&
&&&&&&&&&&&&&&&&&&&&&&&&&&&&&&&&&
&&&&&&&&&&&&&&&&&&&&&&&&&&&&&&&&&

&&&

(unsäglich zu entwirrn)

—Rainer Maria Rilke

&&&&&&&&&&&&&&&&&&&&&&&&&&&&&&&&&
&&&&&&&&&&&&&&&&&&&&&&&&&&&&&&&&&
&&&&&&&&&&&&&&&&&&&&&&&&&&&&&&&&&

How To Read This

This crumpled draft's kindling for an updraft.
Expect the lit candle to arrive by Tuesday
padded envelope color & scent of smoke
curled at the corners & hot.

DO NOT BEND

Carefully unwrap & array the flames
till they cast this spiderweb scribble
back to lithic shadow.

When the candle grows ripe
feed it my tongue.

How To Find Redemption

Paused freight hums on the trestle.
Weak light like it's coming through
an auto body shop's smoky panes.
Windchimes clang like they're pissed
almost as ripped as the frantic flap
of two ragged American flags chained
to the back of an F150's cab.
Vultures nest atop powerline poles.
Who'd join a Masonic lodge
with such crooked brickwork?
Yard statuettes are all
lugubrious little plaster captives.
Even the lusty piping satyr is pale & limp
waiting for his lawyer to call him back.
I drive past the Redemption Center
but they keep piling up in my mud room
garbage bags bulging
with what I've emptied
left unredeemed.
The path I hacked in June down
the embankment to the Deerfield
overgrown with strangling bittersweet
& fat bars of knotweed.
A wailing in the woods, getting closer
a frayed bow sawing, parched for rosin.

How To Perform Miracles & Make Wishes Come True

Someone used to steal the Baby Jesus each year out of the crèche in the town common because who doesn't want a miracle, even a small hollow stolen miracle? Then they attached Jesus to the manger, chain across his infant torso concealed beneath the swaddling. But everyone knows once you chain a god it won't be long before you crucify them.

Wishing's a mostly harmless scratching at unreachable itches, though some wishes are fishhooks snarled deep in my eye. Best to wish simply: wish I didn't lose so many warm gloves, wish I'd just stop stepping on my own improvised explosive devices. Wish my friends less shoelace caught in bike chain wipeouts, less hearts mulched by the chipper, more tacos, forests & portable miracles. I wish you all
all the happiness in the multiverse.

How To Deliver Our Elevator Pitch

Hear that? A something is
singing me, defying pitch, making
me strain for stupid high notes it *knows*
I can't hit. I'll bet there's a sadistic something
singing you too, dimming the Cosmic Microwave
Background, breaking your gravities in half. Please
listen carefully as our menu options become a 30-sec
call waiting static-jangle looped for two hours & thirty-
seven minutes. It smells of burning knuckle hair. It's the 4th
day of July & there's a lot of America happening tonight, loudly.
There are permanent stains on my stainless steel, a blood red
smudge on your timecard. Our greasy hood vent's about
to catch fire. Friday's varnish day at the coffin factory.
Let's dip before we're shitcanned. Let's erode & sell
our wisdom teeth to Alchemy, snip barbed wire
like defector film stars, machete-hack a path
through an absurdly dubbed fever swamp.
Fuck you Oberon, we'll never pimp
out our changeling child.

How To Raise Your Action

When brain's thick milkshake, suck it slow through a straw. Thick Brain say drink all whisky alone. *I'm sorry, Danielle, that may be beyond my abilities right now* is what the sorcerer said when I asked her to stop my buzzing. If your frets buzz you gotta raise your action. To hang a piñata or drain a deer make sure rope's long enough but not too long & strong. To insulate a basement fill the rim joists with rolls of happy pink foam. If brain's chunky coleslaw gone moldy you just have to compost it & hope. To replace a janky garage door measure the rough opening to within a sixteenth. To raise your action insert Allen into truss rod & turn slowly clockwise, quarter inch to start. Too fast or far & it'll crack & your neck's fucked forever. To get some action, try a good pickup line *Wanna dance with me till World War III?* To dance, don't move as though afraid of breaking things, shake ass assuming it's all already broken. Once, totally lost, I shouted at the sorcerer inside my cell *Is forward whichever way I'm going?*

How To Get On First Base

Crunch of dead leaves beneath boots
        first of October
sun's lit saber swoops the treetops
        slashing at eyes

I can list all the things I did today
        but lost track
of all the things that did me
        the one who walks to places

though I don't belong to any of them
        Eunice Williams Drive's
fresh paved tar mist smolders & already striped
        with a streak of struck possum

A maple fell all the way across Green River
        & at Murphy Park Katie hit
a triple & then Autumn got on first base
        primed to steal second

Even though there is no you for me
        still there's this place
I'd love to take you
        I've only ever been here alone

The Secret Stream I call it
        though there's strangers'
sparkly graffiti
        all over the stones

Maybe we could wade in
        or even slip below the cool
surfaces before
        all the leaves die

How To Approach A Swan

Don't. The swans see us for the make believes we are. The swans are Barton Cove's docents & we are refurbished fog machines, doomed swamsuited fops pulled screaming on plastic tubes.

a swan hearts her neck

with another swan's

you should not be watching

it is not for you to see this

The swans cruise through the reeds past glum teens texting on stepdad's gurgling Aqua Patio. The swans are gliding through mist, eliding a jetski's wake.

A young swan family is the Cove's ellipsis, stitching river to sky…

The swans are winning & improving. Their cygnets are floating past our virus. The swans are feathered & buoyant. The swans are contiguous & concurrent. The swans are not sunburned or rueful. The swans are leaving & returning. The swans are dabbling for fish. The swans are

Do the swans sleep

on that island?

Is SWANS! the password

for God's sublime wifi?

Does a sleeping swan slide

behind silence?

How To Light A Candle

for Dave & Lois

This winter mice ate the candles on my porch,
left only shit & wicks. Of course
starving polar explorers ate candles & leather
before consuming each other.
Were my porch mice driven by starvation?
Are certain waxes a delicacy?

When mom's wax was waning, mostly
melted, she took a candle
off the kitchen table & bit
into it before my brother stopped her.
Luckily unlit.

Then forgot how to eat.
I tried feeding her ripped up cold cuts,
pale strips of pink ham,
pantomimed vigorous chewing.
She spit it back in my hand.

Wish I knew how to return
the incandescence she infused in me, last
of six, doctor predicted another
miscarriage. She said dimples were where
the angels kissed her *miracle baby*
grown old, all miracles long used up.

I should light a tall candle,
recite each verse she underlined, incant
words that weigh more than this. She'd ask
why it didn't rhyme. She'd laugh & ask why
I was writing about it
instead of setting mouse traps on my porch.

How To Give It A Name, 3

Columbine used to be the name of a flower. The red, blue, & white starred flag used to be a symbol that represented the United States of America. My pick for Civil War/zombie apocalypse stronghold is the big blue house on Colrain with turrets, stockade fencing, & a gully on three sides we could fill with spikes & fire. Cain really killed Abel because they were in love with the same sister. He became the first funeral caterer & wedding singer. In addition to fratricide he named almost as many things as his parents did. (A name is a solution to a problem it created, said the snake.) Between seven forty & eight thirty-five the air was perfect & for once the sunset was for me. But I set it free to slip off into its last pinks, above a collusion of upended shopping carts sinking into the riverbed.

How To Pronounce My Name

If your name ends
in sibilance people may decide
you don't get your *s* unless
they see you twice
or meet you
& your sister at the same time.
They may impose apostrophes on you—"air
commas" a student called them—
that you don't own or need.
If your name contains
an *l* they may see an *i*
but why do so many want it to be a *y*
turn hailstones into hay bales?
This morning we were talking about…
something interesting, I guess
while I got dressed & I forgot
to put on my belt
spent the rest of the day re-
adjusting my waistline
waisting little notches
of time realigning my midriff
slowing the spooling drift
of my lower half
floorward.
We wear our swervy words
till they've worn us
out, forget they're just so
many wounded sounds
weighed down
by our shifting hourly wants
always failing
shorter, leave lips
key-tap tips, with new
surplus desires to spend us
depend on us

for more mistakes. Daniel
steps to the curb & hales
a cab that's already
passing, already
has three passengers.

How To Get A Promotion

The Chancellor of Lanyards & the Provost of Bolos were traveling incognito as a couple on honeymoon, but this was no suntanning Riviera vaycay. They were attending a covert consortium in Sozopol. The Exchequer of Epaulets was disguised as maître d' at the bistro where they dined & colloquied each evening via reverse semaphore with the Viceroy of Ascots & a revolving cohort of other international power brokers. The bistro was famous for eavesdroppers & assassins in the employ of the Archduchess of Geegaws: beware their exquisite hearing trumpets & poison corsages.

The Chancellor looked positively civilian in her razzle dazzle evening gown… if it weren't for her ceremonial scimitar in bejeweled scabbard. For this vain faux pas & other ontological indiscretions she was canceled, though she went on pretending to be an independent clause, a valid sentence extant beyond revoked title & privilege. (Within a year, however, she'd become one of the Archduchess's assassins.) The Provost even burned down Rhonda's bouncy castle. Which smelled horrible & was excessive since a few punctures would've sufficed, but Burning looked better on his CV.

How To Resign

The soft
opening
for our
Zone
Defense
had the
cringiest
war
-drobe
mal-
function
Kill
adjacent
Tits
deflated
Headshot
hit on
Implicit
Energy
Of Our
Brand
further
defuncted
by
impactful
puff
pieces
cooked
stats
& our
cortège
brutally
Rickrolled
& stirrup

dragged
There
-fore
please
accept my
resignation
as
Chief
Inspiration
Officer.

How To Win The Spring Offensive

The peepers have been peeping for regime change since March. Now the blitz of overgenerous trees, krieg of cottoncandy pollenclouds chokes sky, frosts rivers, clots puddles, every crevice, driveway cracks teeming with weeds, cracks in me, gumming up already sticky levers. Snakes find foundation fissures, chill in my cellar. Everything *too* alive & determined to propagate & trees smell like tantric sex. Lilac isn't a bush, tree, scent, it's a hallucinogenic drug promising impossibilities. Spring's Solid Gold Dancers—primped in Queen Anne's lace, pink poppy spandex, purpled heather boas—say surrender to the sneezy fever dream, sink into a buzzing meadow redolent of yellow unrest, snort a line of pure uncut pollen, invite bugs to commit suicide by flying straight into my eyeballs.

How To Break Answers

They say if it ain't broken
what are you waiting for?
They say cobwebs come
to those who wait.
They say haste makes
hay while the sun is high.
They say if the answer
was a snake it would've
kissed you twice.

How To Exceed Impossible Expectations

&

In a constantly expanding universe we're all getting smaller everyday. But you & I made gnarly stains on the bedcover, sheets, & pillowcases that even the expensive detergent can't get out. (They say *but* erases what came before it, but maybe there's a life after erasure

&&

Your firm emails—flush with ominous innuendo & implied ultra-violence—are not merit-less, but have you tried enhanced interrogation? Between questions, threats, lashes, chew cubes of hospital ice like a savage, grind & crunch the arctic between your eyeteeth.

&&&

Leap headfirst into the quicksand. Don't be a casualty in the war between fog & mist! Fall in the dunk tank even when they miss. Stomp every frozen puddle. In February most calendars are fifty percent off. Get verified as human by every website. It's not too late to change your motto until they embroider it on your collar. No one's guaranteed a sequel. Sister, you're lucky if you get a pilot episode. Save up tears in foil gum wrappers, you'll need them again soon.

&&&&

Bring a cherry pie to a knife fight. *Do Not Walk Outside This Area* is stenciled on the airplane's wing.

&&&&&

She may have been a pastor's wife but Franny loved turning POISON first, then hunting us all down, one by one, & mallet whacking our croquet balls into the neighbor's yard. Her laugh of rapturous triumph, the exceptional light gushing from her eyes.

&&&&&&

As a kid I stole fireflies' glow, smeared luminous soulflesh on face & arms. Catch glints of my ancient fireflecks when jacket zipper gets stuck & I must crawl out backwards like a caterpillar shedding cocoon.

&&&&&&

Upon depletion rest head on desk
& never lift again.

&&&&&&&&

Evening is evening out
the day's great expectations
wouldn't you rather alchemize into
some exotic flower's mancandy
than be a rented mannequin
with a bulbous cyst you have to drain
each summer
it's easier to talk
to strangers then
to walk around
the backyard
naked at night
jiggling the dark breezes

How To Pray

Like Emily
I prefer
wearing all white.
I don't know her

Reasons – mine?
spot intrepid ticks
before they discover
the shore of my skin.

My grieving diet?
Salty chips, a stale crumb
of Hope – yes –
feathered, untethered,

but when scraps
don't sate it – a razor-
beaked Thing
singing beautifully

damning homilies
whose harpy
sharp talons flay,
prey on my heart.

One dead day
I prayed to her
 – no stranger
than genuflecting

to a Virgin Mother,
another arrayed in white –
set alight – ravished
by the sublime.

I halve my communion
crumb. One's enough
for you – a Nobody like
me can subsist on two.

&&&&&&&&&&&&&&&&&&&&&&&&&&&&&&&&&
&&&&&&&&&&&&&&&&&&&&&&&&&&&&&&&&&

&&

(it is impossible to untangle the threads)

—Rainer Maria Rilke, translated by Robert Bly

&&&&&&&&&&&&&&&&&&&&&&&&&&&&&&&&&
&&&&&&&&&&&&&&&&&&&&&&&&&&&&&&&&&

How To Make A New Year's Resolution

Was Jesus ever innocent
even as a manger baby
knowing he was not only son of God
but a third of God themself?
Once I tried talking
to him in my head while doing sit-ups
but it felt a little too awkward
to be called praying.
Often I pray
at myself *please don't do the dumb thing*
even as I bonket cranium
on a left-open cupboard door
spin mud in ravines of
tear-fogged texts I can never unsend
wreckage I can't unwreck
dishes full of broken sink.
Hating on myself is the least
I can do… or is it the most?
Salary & benefits, a joke
but no one else applied.
Even though most houses are still jolly
with twinkling Christmas lights
the House Of Corrections
is the brightest in town.
Abrupt flurries fall like grated manna.
My neighbor's ornament
-stripped pine dragged
stump first to the curb

stray snagged tinsel wisp pulled taut by the wind.

How To Make A Sandwich, 2

Do not drown your brain with math, you only need two slices of bread to begin.

Between the bread, place your most favorite ingredients. Forgo unfavorite ingredients, such as raw or cooked sewage, if you would like your sandwich to be delicious. Don't hack off your foot for funky protein. You can smear pungent blue cheeses on flatbread. Don't sob into your sandwich. Tears dilute the spicy mustard. Fiduciaries & tailored wealth managers concur: avocados & crunchy sprouts are sounder nutritional investments than despair's tetanus boxsprings.

This is not a drill. Nor is it an emergency. It is a sandwich, to be made & enjoyed.

I may not be pretty as a pompadoured crooner in a frilly tux shirt or wise as the wizard with the tallest hat. Perhaps they're all right & I am nothing more than a foolish child zipping a remote control monster truck around the motel parking lot & kicking up a lot of dust, so what do I know about anything, but I like a lot of pickles in a sandwich.

How To Disenchant A Passerine

At 10,000 feet the city's a lit circuit-board
and we're just gribbles gnawing on concrete pilings
which doesn't keep me from showing up sometimes
in the background of stranger's holiday photos
or as an extra in a claymation Christmas special.
I'm nobody, but another nobody loved me.

A lot of people, their dog's the only nice thing about them.
We are a badly botched alchemy experiment
our cracked cauldron melting the icecaps.
I'm just the frog that only sings when no one else can hear.
I'm nobody, who are you?
I'm the starling that started the whole murmuration.

How To Make A Sandwich, 1

Instead of nailing yourself inside your coffin, why not try adding baby arugula & sweet pepper relish to your sandwich?

How To Pass Through Walls

Compose in frequencies

    only dogs can hear

        a leap

            of thinnest listen

                & believe they're there

How To Play

Do not
        out your indoors voices with undue processes
        or eat the waxy slice of cake where the candles melted
        that's the birthday girl's
Do
        howl down the tornado slide
        Sky hard till swing's swung high as will kicking swang
Splay
        out whatever passes through
        Toot your crooked oboe full
        invest your whole held breath in it
Pretend
        you can bend bricks without breaking &
Defend
        your playground from fake pretenders
        unless they're really unreal
Play hard
        & soft
Play
        & play like your playground depends on it

How To Fulfill The Prophecy

There's been another wave of layoffs at the Crater Factory. Elegant custom craters crafted by master craterists are too spendy. Many consumers are watching instructional videos & making their own or simply ordering prefab craters online. The imported craters in the endcap at Target are so cheap, even a family on welfare can afford nice off-brand tax-deductible craters. ("Naturally formed craters"—those supposedly caused by meteorites, ice shelves & tectonics—were seized by the government & shut down years ago.)

When a family moves they often take favorite craters with them, though shipping crates for craters aren't cheap (+ shipping & handling). If your yard comes pre-cratered, you can always remodel, but the old crater's distinct contours inevitably re-emerge in the spring. Best to rubble them & install your own. Some lost craters are irreplaceable, but we try filling them with dozens of smaller craters. (Remember to submit an updated list of total household craters with each census.)

Have you found it yet, has it found you: your true & only fated crater? Do you pray each day to the Greater Crater that is both above & below, the hole so whole it has no top nor bottom?

How To Disappear Completely

      Only
sinking

         sixteen snores
  deep

             beneath
        zipped lids

         starts to
       unsee these

             wavy floaters
               weaving

                     translucent
                     lily pads

        drifting

                wiry tadpoles
                 wriggling

    between
     my

            oblivions

How To Give It A Name, 2

&

Monsoon rain another way of saying *Déjà vu*
the dead don't just get the last word, they get the first word too.

&&

Amidst is filled with a thick sticky mist… it's spilling out all over you. The trick is stuffing the crews' ears with wax & tying your mist to the mast before the sirens start singing

&&&

You know how a bunch of random kids will play at the beach for hours, shouting out

Marco?

Polo!

& never even learn each other's names?

How To Haunt Your House

It only takes one of her hairs on the bedside table

one of her Fat Cat doodles on a Post It

an expired can of whipped cream on the bottom shelf of the fridge

fleece blanket crumpled just so on the futon

Whether it floats flickers or drags chains & moans

a ghost implodes in context

haunts a house that is ready to be haunted

How To Tie & Untie

Some days I don't want the clown to twist me a balloon poodle. Sometimes I don't wanna buy the sugar-water the adorable frantically waving children are selling at their overpriced lemonade stand. If Bandanna Man is standing outside Fosters with his chihuahua in a baby stroller, the law of reentry dictates he cannot roll it back onstage at the start of the next scene. Sometimes sirens sound so unsure of themselves when they first start up, wuh what? I'm constantly amazed that billions of humans are brave & reckless enough to make more humans, especially since so many people hate their own eyebrows. Other days I imagine the clown tying a balloon poodle for the unmade human I almost made with you.

How To Bow Your Heart

For Hannah Fate Wells & Lucas Neal Miller, August 6th 2016

Hannah is a palindrome
Lucas must be fretless strings.

Maybe I should bow to all of you before I sing
out such bold & reckless things?

If Hannah lands in Australia
love says Luke should land there too. Fate agrees
& Sydney too.

Draw a hank of rosined horsehair across their love
louder than four gut strings being bowed.

Bow before love, lovers.
Bow before all the love you have to give each other.

Fate chose a tower that looks out over the Moldau
(or was it a lucky fluke) as the right place for Luke to bow

his heart to Hannah
—that is, Lucas Neal knelt and held the future toward her—

Hannah bows her heart's strings
back to Luke

a symphony *con bravura* enough to promise
Forever.

How To Tie & Untie A Tie

for Deb, Dar, Di, & Donna

The embankment must be graded & graveled before they can lay tracks & hammer in the ties, before the train can bring lumber, power strips, & haberdasher's supplies. One sister, maybe Deb? showed me how to tie a tie, though I never saw any sister wear one, unless Donna, wearing a tie as a bandanna to a Dead show. (No, I don't have a favorite sister; it's a four-way tie.) Honestly the tying isn't as hard as the knotting, the knowing which knot to use to be tight but not *too* tight to untie. It's hard to tie someone else's tie unless you stand behind them. You have to sort of hug them, which for some sad guys might be the first time they hug their Best Man. Groom stands behind bride when blindfolding her, before she tosses bouquet over shoulder & he throws her garter. I didn't see the garter snake in the path until I'd run it over with my bike. I circled back & snake was crossed in a bow & I thought it was done for. But then it undid itself & unraveled like a skinny tie into the bracken. Me, also twisted & broken in here but still not too tangled to unscroll & slither off in the weeds.

How To Climb The Pine At The End Of The Mind

There used to be a HoJos & a mini-golf where the Applebees is.
Linda's house used to be a parsonage
& it said on the deed you weren't allowed to drink booze there.
The bike path used to be train tracks.
The homeless encampment past the tracks
used to be a thicker thicket.
The vacant lot that will soon be McGovern's Ford dealership
used to be a long succession of seedy motels
but for now it's a pile of rubble
like a city that used to be called Mariupol.
What did this shade of blue
used to be before the Prussians claimed it?
The big backyards on Meadow Lane used to be one gigantic meadow.
The Green River Swimming & Recreation Area
used to be the battlefield where that asshole Turner got whomped.
My house used to be our house.
The air around me used to look vacant
before this shock of startled flurries.
The snow-tipped pine corpse at the curb
used to be a succulent *cocus nucifera* swaying in the swelter on the edge
of space, a high cluster of ripe coconuts waiting.

How To Secure The Perimeter

I like the ferns but have decided they're no longer allowed to touch the house. Which you have to admit is perfectly reasonable. I hear a sudden waterfall: my neighbor Jean has turned on her air conditioner. Maybe drowning in this cresting wave of daylilies will stab a hole in my slow sticky air. That vacuum cleaner in the free pile backwashed soon as I turned it on, made my whole house smell like sad wet dog. Do you ever cringe preemptively? I didn't see the cute librarian's wedding ring until I was asking her out. Some people pretend they aren't addicted to air, put NO FEAR stickers on their trucks to prove they aren't scared. Not me. A week ago I cut them back, but some goddam ferns are already touching my porch again.

How To Become An Ornitheologist

Watch avians

build ingenious mangers
    in our dystopian topiary

    robins weave shreds of

blue tarp & cat fur
    into their holy of holies

    hummingbirds drink

communion wine
    from hosta trumpets.

Hear the bird

    that sounds like
a tap left running

hear the bird

    sounds like
a defibrillator?

    Consign prayers

to birds
    migrating north

    geese see god

greet her with
    solemn honks.

How To Die

Come back as a tree. There's no better way to learn how to leave.
Be a sugar maple, sob out all your sap each spring.

How To Be Mist

The oxbow's glassed over with cold. Windows shiver their panes. The plows are coming later this winter, roads keep growing narrower, which doesn't stop a pair of young lovers from strolling past Scrooge's house in papier mâché jackets, characters in a Hallmark movie where there's no black slush, no scenes set in snowdrifting graveyards. The tombstones are iceberged in a frozen sea… except for two old slate stones that lean toward each other. So old, names are gone, leaning so close they're nearly touching. Between them, the snow's melted, brown earth exposed. In the made-for-tv movie, their spectral cartilage is fused for eternity.

One August night, big orange moon, the week before college, I climbed cemetery gates with two friends & hurried down stone rows to a pond in the center of the graveyard. We paddled an inflated raft out to a small misty island. All we accomplished was waking the ducks & swans that slept there, but when you're eighteen & about to leave home you can row past the dead, wake their winged guardians, & still walk home wet, laughing & half immortal. By now I should know, be more ready to go, but no. Forgive this most sentimental, superficial wish: to be mist. I want to be mist by you. I want to be mist *on* you. Mist on your hands and face. Mist that dissolves on your tongue & lips.

How To Unread This

This tattoo is for lovers & doctors
skin on loan to taxidermy interns
owl-haunted silo enrobed in kudzu
stained glass window that opens all the way
bend beyond where candle eats wick's end

&&&&&&&&&&&&&&&

&

it is impossible to

translate

&&&&&&&&&&&&&&&&

Re   This

This   rumpled   raft's
               lit

                              &

                                  the flames

                  shadow

                              rows
            my tongue

Red   ion

a

      ripped
     ragged

          brick

  the

        Red   ion

       emptied
 unred

    a
       strangling
      knot
  a   loser
a frayed   wing

How To   live

Hear

    rain
     hit
             the
  ground break   your   lease

      smell
            America   a   loud
           greasy
  fire
              erode
like
   an absurd
            imp
 o r   angel

First

    first
        swoop   to
    slash

all the

      mist

        second

        place

          a

  Secret

spark

       below

    the eaves

Approach

Don't   make

                                                  fog

with another

               be

mist

                                                 or

   the

                  sword

behind silence

and

O
and her

ice

melted and

Then
her old
mime
spit back

each
word

Re

open
    our

war
-drobe

  its

  on

Brand

  fun

&

brutal

&

Leap   into the
        mist!

                    It's   too late to
                                            ante
                                        up tears

A New   solution

Jesus

   tried talking
   in my head
    a little   war
  called praying.
   I pray

in   a
   fog

    of   sin
    my

      name
ripped   ragged

   nagged   by the wind

How To   appear Complete

      Only
inking

         the

                    lucent

           rift

    between
    my

            ions

&&

                                        mist... it's
    you. The   ax
            is   art

&&&

    how   will
each hour

  arc

&   earn   her name ?

Mist

The   bow's   heir
                        is   arrow

touching   the   now's
                                      used   eternity

One

mist   is   king
                                                            can
                                                            we
                                                    read
                this   mist
                            mist   Mist
Mist that dissolves   our tongue & lips

This

This   too is   over
skin   a
    haunted   robe
a   glass   hat pens   the
end beyond   end

Who To Thank

Thank you to the editors of the journals where some of these poems first appeared:

ballast
Conduit
Hush
Meat For Tea
The Montague Reporter
#Ranger
Upender
Write Action: Poems Around Town

Love, thanks, & tacos to:

CA for sharing the hidden rose & the fine art of Spite & Malice
Corwin, Earl, & Sally for invaluable mist-wrangling assistance
J Lowe, Brian, & Ol Brandon for transcendental heaving
The Wells Millers for dragon rows & rosin on my bow
The Wild Millers for ropeswing bliss & garlic braids
& you for reading & unreading this twisted mist

Who To Blame

Daniel Hales is the author of the hybrid novel *Run Story* (Shape&Nature Press), the poetry collection *¿Cómo Hacer Preguntas? or How To Make Questions: 69 Instructional Poems In English* (Frayed Edge), & three poetry chapbooks: *Shake My Ashes* (Beard of Bees), *Blind Drive* (White Knuckle), & *Tempo Maps* (Ixnay). His writing has appeared in *Booth, Conduit, The Massachusetts Review, Quarter After Eight,* & elsewhere. He makes music as Umbral, The Ambiguities, & Selah haleS. The most recent album by his band, The Frost Heaves & Hales, is *Ghost Of A Chance To The Shadow Of A Doubt*. His preferred place of worship is a kayak. His sensei is The Cat Of Many Names.

www.danielhales.com

More from Frayed Edge Press

More Poetry!

House of Jars by Hester L. Furey
The Ghettobirds by Bryant O'Hara
¿Cómo Hacer Preguntas? or How To Make Questions: 69 Instructional Poems in English by Daniel Hales
The Splooge Factory by Christina Springer

More Fiction!

The Flying African by Areg Azatyan; translated by Nazareth Seferian
Blessed Hands: Stories by Frume Halpern; translated by Yermiyahu Ahron Taub
Loose in the Bright Fantastic by E.B. Moore
Songs for the Gusle by Prosper Mérimée; translated by Laura Nagle
Street Smart X 7 : A Street Smart Series Omnibus edited by Alison M. Lewis
DIG by Robert Paul Moreira
In Madison's Cave: A Novel by Douglas Anderson
Yearning for the Sea by Esther Seligson; translated by Selma Marks
Ambushing the Void by James McAdams
Bellapalma by Jens Bjørneboe; translated by Esther Greenleaf Mürer
Ere the Cock Crows by Jens Bjørneboe; translated and with a reconstruction of the play by Esther Greenleaf Mürer
Right Guy, Wrong Time by Louise MacGregor
Stealing: A Novel in Dreams by Shelly Brivic

More History and Politics!

"Do Not Misunderstand Me": The Collected Radical Addresses to the Unity Congregation (1888-1891) by Hugh Owen Pentecost, edited by Robert P. Helms
Jeremiah Hacker: Journalist, Anarchist, Abolitionist by Rebecca Pritchard
A Nurse's Story: Medical Missionary in Korea and Siberia, 1915-1920 by Delia Battles Lewis

Forthcoming!

Werewolf Movie by Stephen St. Francis Decky (novel)
Silent Cauldron by E.B. Moore (novel)
Our Dad the Commie by John Oliver Hodges (biography/memoir)
Dwelling in Time by Esther Seligson; translated by Selma Marks (fiction)
Music the World Makes by John Loonam (novel)

Visit us at: https://www.frayededgepress.com/